Poems N
Never Hear

Jemima Naylor

Poems Nobody Will Never Hear © 2022
Jemima Naylor

All rights reserved.

Presentation by *BookLeaf Publishing*

Web: www.bookleafpub.com

E-mail: info@bookleafpub.com

ISBN: 978-93-95950-17-6

First edition 2022

ACKNOWLEDGEMENT

To my friends and family for listening to the ramblings of a mad woman and enjoying it.

i love you

_experiences

If you are lucky enough,
Travel the world
I'm telling you to do it
Don't hesitate, don't wait.
Just do
I swear it'll be the best thing you've ever done.

Dance under the stars
Get sand in unwanted places
Feel the warmth of sun burn on your cheeks
Eat foods that you can't even pronounce
Make friends
Find love
Do whatever the hell you want
But do it somewhere different
Because the confinement of the four walls
In your small town
Will act as a cage
And you can only grow so much as there is
room

Re-read this when you are home.
Did you travel the world?
Did you hesitate? Did you wait?
Did you do?
Was it the best thing you've ever done?

If yes,
What are you waiting for
Do it again.

_my biggest inspiration

a woman,
a friend,
a wife,
a mother
a boss,
a shoulder;
All these different people,
She lives in different ways
I'm glad I got to experience her
So close to me,
Sorry to the passerby's who may only get her
smile
You're missing out on the something magic
Of having her in your life

_Naughty Child

A fear so great
He didn't leave a corner for 17 hours
But he was a 'naughty child'
A dad so useless the abuse was allowed
A stepmother so evil she gained pleasure from
his pain
Is humanity to blame?
Or is she one individual
Who is clearly mentally insane.

A mothers nature is to love and care
But this has happened so many times before
Another child has died from severe abuse
But who really deserves it, tell the truth…

The stepmother?
The dad?
The school?
The community?
Or social services?
The blame list is endless

But does it even matter now
He's dead, they're in prison.
How did it ever get to this stage

Outraged.
Disgusted
Damn right sick
A boy aged 6
Stuck in time
His future, what future?
A boy so scared he stayed in a corner for 17
hours.

_The Sun in the Sky

She beamed;
And she knew then
This is where she was meant to be.

_No Body Attached

Sex
Wonderful, mysterious, an intimate act
I love it so much
I'm an addict at heart

Sex
Pain, lies, an intimate act
Is it for love or pleasure
They're both pretty jacked

Sex
I want it, I get it, an intimate act
I don't even like the guy
Fuck, isn't that bad?

Sex
Natural, feel good, an intimate act
Shit he loves me
I don't love him back.

Sex
I use him, play him for this intimate act
I guess that's over now
He's figured me out

Sex
Now I gotta get back on track
To find someone for the intimate act
This one lasted longer than the others
Are triple AAA batteries the best ones for that?

_Front Door

The day we bought our house
Was the best day
And me and you were finally
A family
I knew that you were the one
For me
As you walked through the front door
Of our home

We lived there for one year
Happily
But I worked too much and
You were lonely
But it was all okay
When you walked through the front door
Of our home

The months passed by so slowly
When our love faded eventually
We were not happy anymore
So I no longer walked
Through your front door

I saw you 5 months later
You were at the bus stop with a girl

I knew then when I looked at you,
You were the one I lost
And I miss you walking through
Our front door

I think about you everyday
Though it's been so long
I know you have a baby on the way
I wish I was carrying yours
And I know that now you have someone else
Walking through your front door

Your wedding looked beautiful
On the photos
And I'm still the same place I've been
You've moved on now and I'm proud
But I hate myself for letting you win
I know you don't think about me anymore
But I still wish
I was the one walking
Through your front door

The first day I didn't think of you
I felt so free, I met somebody
He had a wonderful soul
And I finally felt like letting go
He became my home
As I walked through his front door

You saw me across the street a few years later on
You smiled and walked across
Your beautiful little girl asked who I was
And you said
I was your home long ago
You at looked at me and saw I was having a
baby
And said you wish it was yours
The memories of our life came flushing in
Of us walking through our front door

We are soulmates I believe it so
But..
Unfortunately you were not the one
Because the one for me
Just walked through my
Front door

_this life I did not choose but have been lucky enough to have

my parents have shown me that love is not
rainbows and sunshine
but that it is hard work
and it hurts
they are the strongest people I have ever met.
and how lucky I am to have been raised by two
individuals who work so well together as one.

my brother who is the happiest person I have
ever met,
but has faced adversity and difficulties that are
unimaginable
and yet his smile, oh, his infectious smile
warms my heart when I see it

my oldest brother, you are so intelligent and so
funny and I am so grateful for this relationship
we share
thank you for being an incredible role model
for me, your annoying baby sister

my little nan, our short time together left an
imprint on my heart
and I wish you were here to see me grow into
the woman I am today.
but a little girl always needs her mummy, and I
wish my mum could have had longer with you.

my big nan, what an incredible woman you are.
and you have been all of my grandparents in
one. which is no easy feat that you have done,
extremely well
i thank you for the huge part you have played in
my life

my family,
how weird, wacky and crazy we may be
you're mine forever, thankfully

_growth

3 years ago we named our group
'A-block girls'
laughter, tears, memories made that'll last a
lifetime. I think it's official now:
a block women.

_A Wish I Made When I Was 4

The lipstick on the mug doesn't belong to me
The jewellery in the drawer is not mine
The clothes in the wardrobe are much too big
The heels are way too high

Oh how I wished to be grown up like her

The lipstick on the mug has come from my lips
The jewellery in the drawer I own
The clothes in the wardrobe are too small
The heels are still too high

Oh wow, how I will try
To explain to my daughter growing up is not all
it's cracked up to be

_The Wolf Pack

The loudest, the leader, the one who's known
Pull her down, drag her down, make sure she's
alone
Our pack has levels
I'm sure your aware
Top dog but her betas
They don't want her there
She needs knocking down a step
Removing from the pedestal
They put her on
It won't be easy
But they think it must be done
Planned in a way
So that it's her idea
Clever, I must say
But fuck that and fuck them
I'm staying here rightfully

Who's next to challenge me

_Do You Have Anything To Say To Me?

Is it anger or
disappointment,
disgust,
shame.
There is definitely no
Pride

I don't feel well
tears fall
Stress is heavier
Back is breaking
Heart is breaking
"Mine or yours?"

You say I am 21
As though that is negative
As though I'm supposed to be fully grown
I'm not
I've still got so much to learn
"You can't do that from being in bed"
You'd reply

I'm sitting here
Taking it all in

And I'm becoming less of myself
Because it is wrong
My behaviour
I have no reason to be sad
"I get everything done for me"
"I laze around in bed"
Your words cut me deep
Deeper than anything I could feel about myself

My head hurts
Feels like another migraine
Now I am convinced they're caused by stress
I'm stressed because I've not done enough?
I'm stressed because I'm not enough?
I'm stressed because I'm not smart enough?
Pretty enough?
Enough!

I'm not supposed to feel this way
I've had a fortunate life
I've been given so much
I am so loved
How can I complain about anything
How fucking ungrateful does that make me
How selfish does that make me

I'm feel as though I'm becoming a shadow of
myself
I'm not like this

I am unapologetically myself
If I am a lot, go and find less
That is the vibe
Period.

But
I can't not care
That isn't me either
I can, not care
When I actually don't care.
But when I do
Oh I fucking do
And I get so annoyed when I don't want to care
Because, I just do.

I don't want you to be angry or
disappointed,
disgusted,
ashamed.
All I want to feel off you is
Pride

Enough.

_Her Housemates

How do I feel so lonely in a house full of people
I love
How do I miss my family when I see them at
least once a month
How do I not have the closest friend
When's theres half a dozen to choose from right
now
And finally how
Do I help myself feel better
About things I cannot change
Oh it's nobody's fault
I feel this way
I wish though I had someone to blame
There's 2 of them and they're so close
It's impossible to even catch up
There's another 3 who are
So 'witchy'
And one who disappeared with no trace
Oh but there is no one to blame
For me feeling this way
I am lonely and alone
In a house full of people
In my own home

Now I'm not always

Sad
Let's remember that fact
I don't always feel this way
When I'm with them
I feel involved
But it's when I'm alone
It begins again
There's nothing to do
And there's no one to blame
For my feelings this way
All I can do is try and push through
By keeping myself involved
With them all
In a house full of people
In my own home

I've kept it to myself for the longest time
I didn't want anyone to know
I wrote how I felt on a note
And added to it
When the feelings came again
There's no one to blame
For me feeling this way
I remind myself time and again
But how did they not realise
I felt this way
In a house full of people
In my own home

_you know what you must do

For a girl who's not meant to be still
You've stayed in one place a long time
Maybe that is why
Your light is dimming inside.

For a girl who is so confident and bubbly
You've been quiet for some time
Maybe you should venture
To find yourself, live your life

For a girl who isn't lost
Your sure seem unable to find your way
I will guide you
You will find your place someday

Home. You know where it is
But you need to flee the nest
Now, my darling
You know that a home is a much better place
When you leave and have somewhere to come
back to

Each path you go
Each road you cross
Live your life

No matter the cost
You know what you must do
Fly my little wild thing,
Fly.

_self love = more love

you fill up her cup
because she's a woman,
she's a friend, she's gone through a lot
but as you fill her up,
don't forget your cup,
she needs you too.

_i love me, who do you love?

why is it called a "first love"
why are we told that our first love is another
person
why is so much importance placed on
your first love in your first relationship
my first love is named jemima naylor
and whoever my second love is, is in for a real
treat because she is fucking awesome.

_An Important Delicacy

You're the only person I truly know.
For me that's the greatest goal.
To know myself is all that counts
To the end, you're my truest friend.

_Constant

Sharing my true feelings
Is something I do
I'm honest, I'm open
I try to remain true

I often feel
The need to remind
The others that I'm not
An empty, numb, hollow being inside

_changing pattern

am I picky
or a commitment-phobe
or not met the right person

age is just a number apparently
so do I need to have found the one
at twenty-one?
i feel that is "what's done"

the fear that I'll be alone forever
is not a big deal
but the fear that I won't be fulfilled
haunts me
i want a full life,
and i want to share it with someone

how do I approach a situation
as such
when it is completely new territory
i have no clue
what I'm doing

do I stick with what is the norm for me
it hasn't worked in the past
maybe something will be different, I hope
though i do believe that is the dictionary

definition of
insane

i enjoy the life I'm living now,
but will I in 5 months time?
why do I feel so comfortable drunk
and uncomfortable sober
I'm confident, I'm happy
but clearly lacking intimacy
bite the fucking bullet
grow a pair of tits

i love to play the worst case scenario game
with other peoples lives
what am I so scared of
there's genuinely no reason;
apart from never having tried it before
but as every adult tells a child
how do you know you don't like something
until you try it

i want to live by that truly
is it easier said than done?
other people seem to do it so easily
when can I be one of those

doesn't the saying go; if I want to change,
always start today.
start today. start today. start today.

_not pathetic! fallacy

Some days you wake up and the sun is shining
Other days the rain is pouring
Some days the snow is so heavy
You cannot leave your house
And others the fog so thick
You cannot see through it

But it's okay, because
Rainy, snowy, foggy days
They clear

Some days you wake up in the greatest mood
Others you want to cry all day
Some days you cannot leave your bed
And others there is a numb pain within your
head

Life is not one type of weather
Nor one feeling
But allowing that to be okay
Is what makes you so great.

_bed

My heart belongs to you
It's where I feel warm
I feel so safe wrapped up in you
My dreams are safe with you
I don't want to leave
Morning or night
I could stay with you all day
And you would not complain
I can lie on top
Or underneath your clothes
you've been there for me
In my lightest and darkest days
I thank you for the rest, that you provide
For the comfort you bring
If I'm alone or with another
You would never leave me
My trust in you does never falter
I'll stay with you till the end
And when the time comes
Even then
I'll lie in one of your friends

_an adventure into the unknown

i want to run, flee, escape
this vulnerability
i feel
i can't help but hate it
i can feel my heart opening and I can't stand it
how do I free fall
when I've no idea if you are going to
catch me